D1573133

Rescue Helicopters

by Becky Olien

Consultant:
Carl Shafer
Executive Director
American Helicopter Museum and Education Center

Bridgestone Books
an imprint of Capstone Press
Mankato, Minnesota

Bridgestone Books are published by Capstone Press
151 Good Counsel Drive, P.O. Box 669, Mankato, Minnesota 56002
http://www.capstone-press.com

Library of Congress Cataloging-in-Publication Data
Olien, Rebecca.
    Rescue helicopters/by Becky Olien.
    p. cm.—(The transportation library)
    Includes bibliographical references and index.
    ISBN 0-7368-0844-2
    1. Helicopters in search and rescue operations—Juvenile literature. 2. Helicopters—Juvenile
literature. [1. Helicopters. 2. Rescue work.] I. Title. II. Series.
TL553.8 .O43 2001
629.133'352—dc21   00-009911

Editorial Credits

Karen L. Daas, editor; Karen Risch, product planning editor; Timothy Halldin, cover designer;
    Erin Scott, illustrator; Heidi Schoof, photo researcher

Photo Credits

Archive Photos, 16
Diane Meyer, 8–9
Lambert/Archive Photos, 12
Popperfoto/Archive Photos, 14–15
Unicorn Stock Photos/Terry Barner, 6
Visuals Unlimited/Steve Strickland, cover, 20; Betty Sederquist, 4; Gerald A. Corsi, 18

1 2 3 4 5 6 06 05 04 03 02 01

Table of Contents

Rescue Helicopters

People use rescue helicopters to help those in danger. Rescue helicopters pick up people who are trapped or hurt. They rescue people from floods, forest fires, earthquakes, and volcanoes. Rescue helicopters also transport injured people to hospitals.

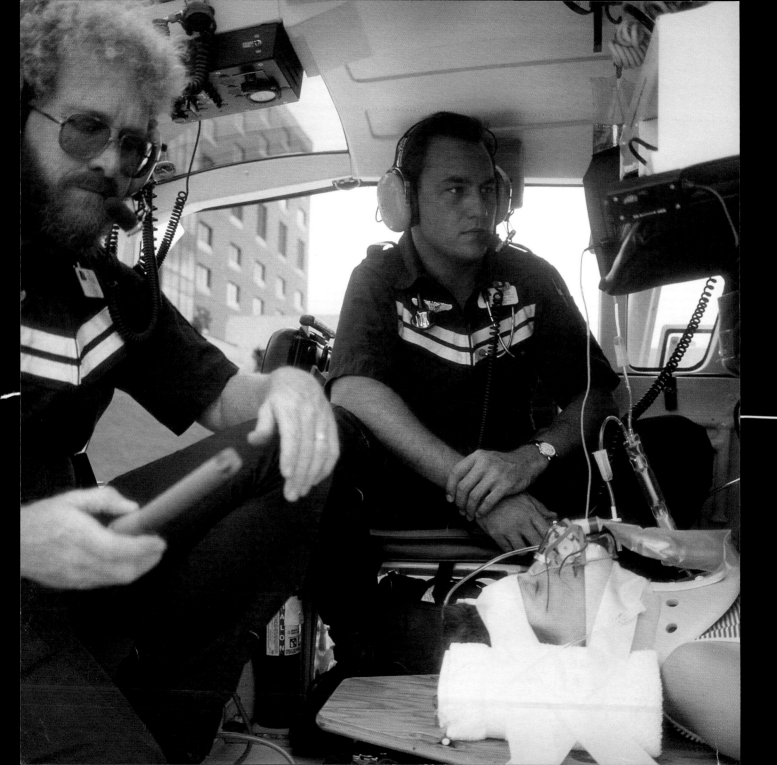

Rescue Helicopter Crews

The members of a rescue helicopter crew work together to help people. The pilot flies the helicopter. The co-pilot helps the pilot navigate. A winchman lowers a cable to people on the ground or in the water. Medics take care of people who are hurt.

medic
a person who is trained to help injured people; paramedics and emergency medical technicians are medics.

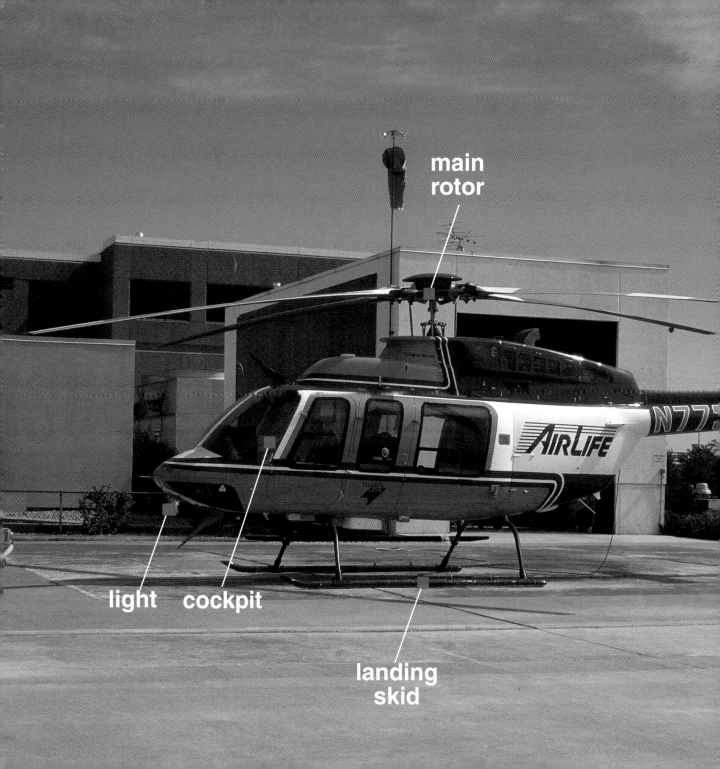

main
rotor

AirLife

N777

light   cockpit

landing
skid

tail
rotor

Parts of a Rescue Helicopter

Some rescue helicopters have a main rotor and a tail rotor. Other rescue helicopters have two large main rotors. Pilots sit in the cockpit. Lights help pilots search for people at night. A rescue helicopter has landing skids or wheels.

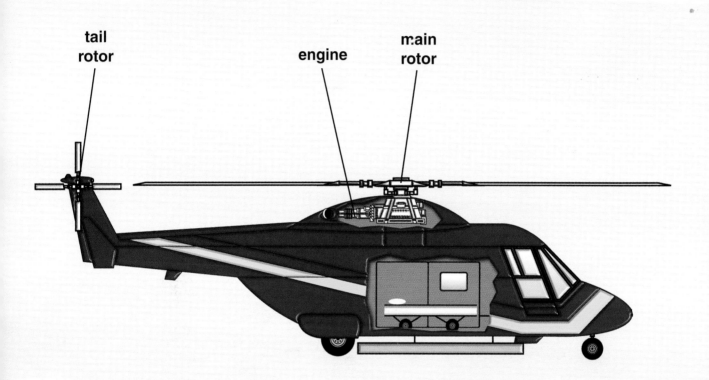

tail
rotor

engine

main
rotor

How a Rescue Helicopter Works

An engine turns a rescue helicopter's rotors. Spinning rotors lift the rescue helicopter into the air. The pilot uses control sticks and pedals. They control the direction and speed of the rescue helicopter. Rescue helicopters also can hover above an area.

hover
to stay in one place in the air

Before the Rescue Helicopter

People used cars, boats, and airplanes to rescue people before the helicopter was invented. But these vehicles often could not reach people in remote places. Many of these people could not be rescued.

remote
hard to reach

Inventors of the Helicopter

In 1907, Paul Cornu of France invented the first helicopter. It stayed in the air for 20 seconds. Igor Sikorsky of Russia invented the first helicopter to fly long distances. He flew his helicopter in the United States in 1939.

Early Rescue Helicopters

Early rescue helicopters did not have much power. They could not carry a heavy load. These helicopters could rescue only one person at a time.

Rescue Helicopters Today

Today, rescue helicopters are larger and faster. They also carry medical equipment. Rescue helicopters use rescue collars or baskets to pick up people. Rescue helicopters transport injured people to hospitals faster than ambulances and boats can.

Rescue Helicopter Facts

- Many hospitals have helipads. Rescue helicopters land on these areas. Hospital workers move the injured people from the rescue helicopter into the hospital.

- The U.S. Coast Guard uses rescue helicopters to help people who are drowning. They also save people from burning or sinking ships.

- The U.S. military rescues injured soldiers with rescue helicopters. The crew lands or lowers a rope or basket to the injured soldier. The crew then lifts the soldier into the rescue helicopter. The crew transports the soldier to a military hospital.

- Rescue helicopter crews save animals as well as people. Crews sometimes rescue farm animals. They also move bears to new homes.

Hands On: Make a Whirly Bird

The first idea for a helicopter came from a flying toy top made in China long ago. Other flying toys helped people invent the helicopter. Some, like this whirly bird, had feathers.

What You Need

3 feathers
A 1-inch (2.5-centimeter) Styrofoam ball
Marker
Toothpick
Plastic straw
A windy day

What You Do

1. Poke the feathers into the Styrofoam ball so they are the same distance apart.
2. Two of the feathers are the bird's wings. The other feather is its tail. Draw a face with a marker between the two wings.
3. Stick the toothpick in the bottom of the ball.
4. Place the toothpick in the end of the plastic straw.
5. Hold the straw up so the whirly bird catches the wind.
6. Watch as the wind lifts the bird from the straw.

The feather wings and tail are like the rotors of a helicopter. As they spin, they lift the bird into the air.

Words to Know

cockpit (KOK-pit)—the area in a rescue helicopter where pilots sit

hover (HUHV-ur)—to stay in one place in the air

medic (MED-ik)—a person who is trained to help injured people; paramedics and emergency medical technicians are medics.

navigate (NAV-uh-gate)—to decide the direction a vehicle should travel

pilot (PYE-luht)—a person who flies a helicopter or other aircraft

transport (transs-PORT)—to move people or goods from one place to another

Read More

Otfinoski, Steven. *Whirling Around: Helicopters Then and Now.* Here We Go! New York: Benchmark Books, 1999.
Rogers, Hal. *Rescue Helicopters.* Rescue Machines at Work. Eden Prairie, Minn.: Child's World, 2000.
Stille, Darlene R. *Helicopters.* A True Book. New York: Children's Press, 1997.

Internet Sites

American Helicopter Museum
http://helicoptermuseum.org
Canadian Museum of Flight
http://www.canadianflight.org
United Technologies—Discovery Center
http://www.utc.com/discover/index.htm

Index